**Project Editor** Sue Grabham
**Senior Contributing Editor** Charlotte Evans
**Assistant Editor** Tara Benson
**Section Editor** Angela Holroyd

**Senior Designer** Janice English
**Section Designer** Ch'en Ling
**Additional Design** Smiljka Surla

**Publishing Director** Jim Miles

**Art Director** Paul Wilkinson

**Additional Art Preparation**
Matthew Gore, Andy Archer, Shaun Deal,
Julian Ewart, Narinder Sahotay, Andy Stanford,
Janet Woronkowicz

**Picture Research** Elaine Willis
**Artwork Archivist** Wendy Allison
**Artwork Researcher** Robert Perry

**Activity Artist** Caroline Jayne Church

**Indexer** Hilary Bird

**Production Manager** Linda Edmonds
**Production Assistant** Stephen Lang

**Contributing Authors**
Christopher Maynard, Jean-Pierre Verdet

**Specialist Consultants**
James Muirden BEd (Publications Consultant
at School of Education, University of Exeter
and astronomy writer);
Julia Stanton BA DipEd (Australasia consultant)

**Educational Consultants**
Ellie Bowden (Curriculum Advisor for
Primary Science and Senior Teacher, Essex);
June Curtis (Primary School Teacher, Nottingham
and R.E. writer);
Kirsty Jack (Head Teacher, Primary
School, Edinburgh)

**KINGFISHER**
An imprint of Larousse plc
Elsley House, 24-30 Great Titchfield Street, London W1P 7AD

First published by Chambers 1994

Reprinted in 1997

Copyright © Larousse plc 1995

A CIP catalogue record for this book is available from the British Library.

ISBN 1 85697 257 7

Typeset by Tradespools Ltd, Frome, Somerset
Colour separation by P&W Graphics, Singapore

 Produced in the E.C.
by *Partenaires-Livres*®
on SCA paper

# Kingfisher Child's World Encyclopedia

People
and
Places
– 10 –

Kingfisher

# Contents

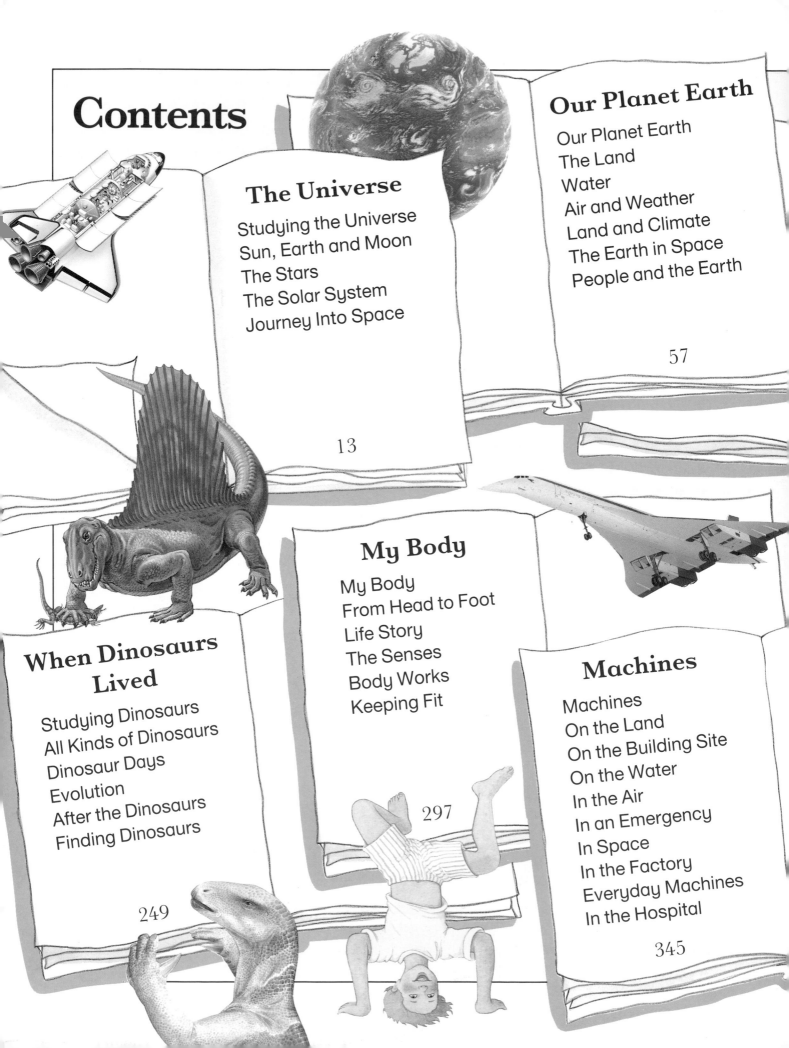

## The Universe

## Our Planet Earth

## When Dinosaurs Lived

## My Body

## Machines

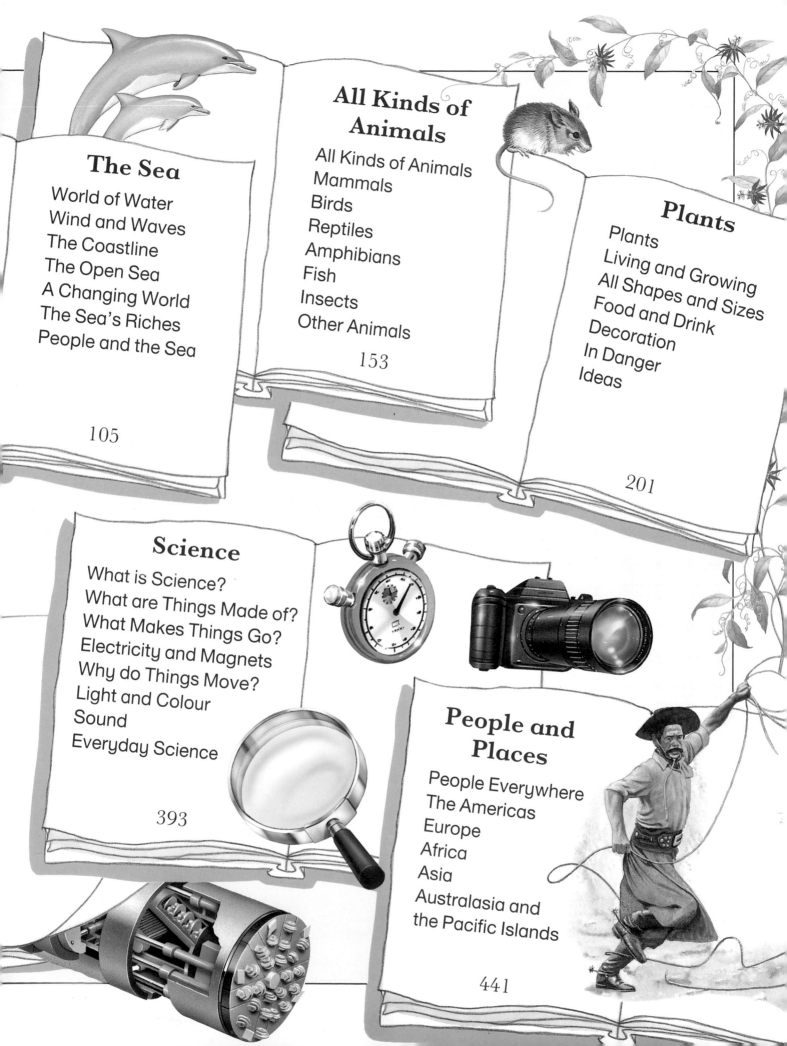

# Activities

Before you start each activity, collect everything you need and make sure there is a clear space. Wash your hands before cooking and wear gloves when touching soil. Wear an apron for gluing, cooking and using paints.
If an adult is needed, ask if they can help before you start.
Afterwards, make sure you clear up any mess and put everything away.

▷ Here are some of the materials that you might need for the activities. **Always** ask an adult before using anything that is not yours.

Recipe

500 g plain flour
150 g salt
1 mug water
food colouring

## Make dough

Make dough for some of the modelling activities. Mix flour and salt in a bowl. If making coloured dough, add food colouring to water. Add as much water as needed to flour and salt, a little at a time. Stir. Turn out onto floured surface. Knead into a smooth dough. Make models. When finished, ask an adult to put them in the oven, on a low heat, for five hours. Paint the models when cool.

# People and Places

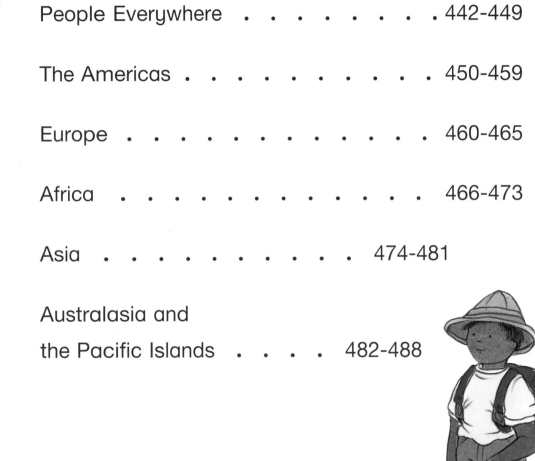

# Where do people live?

The world we live in is made up of many different environments, or surroundings. These include deserts, grasslands, woodlands, rainforests and mountains. Some of these areas are shown on the map. People can live in almost every area.

Since early times, people have built homes with natural materials that grew or were found close by. Today, many homes are built with materials made in factories.

▽ Inuit people in North America used igloos as homes. Igloos were built of blocks of snow.

**Key to map**

|  |  |  |  |
|---|---|---|---|
| | hot desert | | evergreen forest |
| | grassland | | deciduous wood |
| | cold desert | | rainforest |
| | | | mountains |

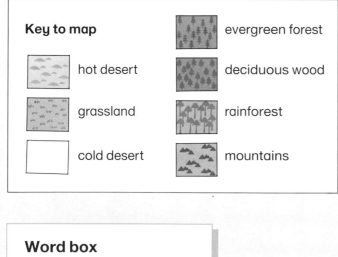

△ People live in reed houses on Lake Titicaca in South America. They are built on a floor of flattened reeds.

**Word box**
**Environments** are our surroundings. They affect the way we live.
**Manufactured** materials are made in a factory.

▽ About 300 years ago, many European homes had thatched roofs made of straw. Thatching is still done today.

**Factory materials**

Materials such as glass, concrete, bricks, steel and strong plastics are used to build homes all over the world. These materials are manufactured, which means they are made in a factory.

△ China has so many people that most city buildings are overcrowded. Some people live on rivers in houseboats.

△ In many parts of Africa, mud and straw are easy to come by. So mud houses with thatched roofs are popular.

△ Australia is an enormous country. People who are travelling across it may live in camper vans for a while.

# Languages

Language is made up of spoken and written words. Without words it would be difficult for us to tell others what we mean. We would have to act out what we were trying to say, which would take a long time. It is hard to understand people from other countries, because they use different words to say the same thing.

**Whispering game**

One player whispers to a neighbour. They repeat what was said to the person next to them, and so on. The last person says it out loud. Usually, the words have changed.

▷Throughout the world, hands are used in different ways as a greeting, and as a sign of welcome and respect.

▽ The children below are all saying good morning. The different languages are written above them. How many do you know?

你好嗎

ঘুসুবেয়ো

günaydın

안녕

Buenos días

おはよう

jamm nga fënaan

नमस्कार

שָׁלוֹם, בֹּקֶר טוֹב

здравствуи

καλημέρα

ကျွတ်ဆောင်းပေါ်မော။

GOOD MORNING

السلام عَلَيْكُم ~ ال

BONJOUR!

# Religious beliefs

Many things have happened in the world that we do not understand. Religious beliefs are one way of helping to explain them. Most religions have a god or gods and laws to tell people how to behave. Some people's special religious buildings are shown here.

△ There are many gods in the Hindu religion. One god, Shiva, is carved on the walls of this Hindu temple.

△ Buddhists follow the sayings of the Buddha. They worship in a temple.

△ In Jerusalem, The Western Wall is visited by Jews, who believe in one god only.

△ Christians worship one god and Jesus Christ in chapels, churches and cathedrals.

△ Shinto symbols are important to Japanese people who worship gods of nature.

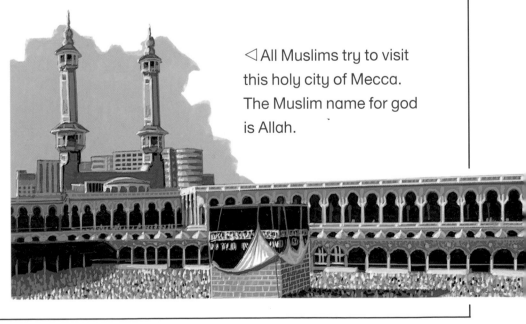

◁ All Muslims try to visit this holy city of Mecca. The Muslim name for god is Allah.

445

# Food from far and wide

All kinds of delicious foods are grown throughout the world. Different types of weather, called climate, help to decide how people live and what sort of food they grow.

Once, certain foods were only eaten by the people who grew them. Today, food can be transported to markets all over the world for us to buy. How many of the foods below do you know?

**Make a fruit salad**
Buy some brightly coloured fruits and wash them. Ask an adult to cut them into cubes and slices. Place in a bowl and mix together. Add a little fresh fruit juice.

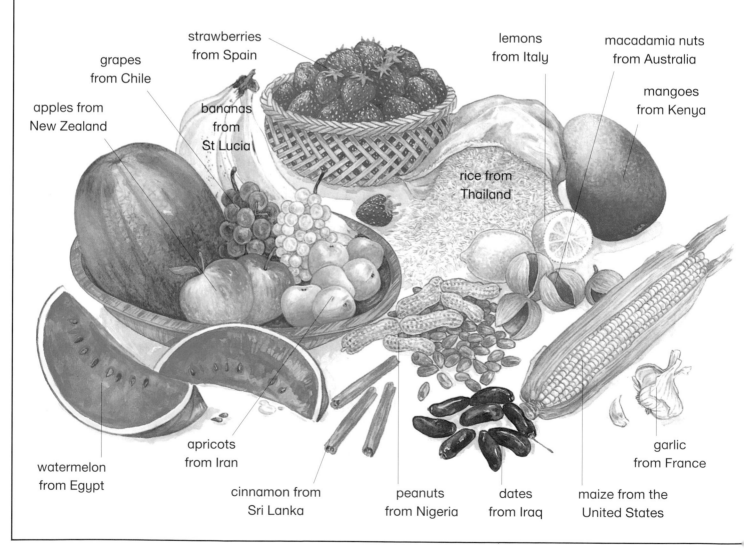

strawberries from Spain

grapes from Chile

lemons from Italy

macadamia nuts from Australia

apples from New Zealand

bananas from St Lucia

mangoes from Kenya

rice from Thailand

watermelon from Egypt

apricots from Iran

cinnamon from Sri Lanka

peanuts from Nigeria

dates from Iraq

maize from the United States

garlic from France

446

# Sports and games

People all over the world play sports and games all through the year. Some are played alone, while others are played with a partner or in teams. Football and hockey are games that are played against people in many countries, to decide which country's team is the winner. Which sports and games do you enjoy playing?

△ Ice hockey is a fast and tough game.

△ Volleyball is played on beaches worldwide.

▽ Every four years, sports men and women from different countries meet to play against each other at the Olympic games. The winners are given medals.

△ In Katanga, Zaire, children play a game of marbles using fruits.

▷ Children and adults all over the world enjoy kicking a ball and playing football.

447

# Traditions

A tradition is something that is done in the same way, year after year. It may be a celebration, a storytelling or a way of making something. Different places and groups of people have their own traditional festivals, stories and crafts.

In the following pages, we will be looking at five large areas of the world: the Americas, Europe, Africa, Asia and Australasia and the Pacific Islands. Each is made up of many countries that all have their own traditions.

△ For thousands of years, African people have made models out of clay, wood and gold. This head is made of red clay. It was made in west Africa about 800 years ago.

◁ Every year, people in Belgium, Europe, dress up as giants for a parade around the town streets. Each costume has a peephole, so the person inside can see where they are going. Can you see the people's faces in this picture?

**Snowmaiden**
(A Russian folk tale)

*Once upon a time, a couple who longed to have a child carved a young girl out of snow. When she magically came alive they were delighted and called her Snowmaiden.*

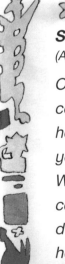

▷These traditional rod puppets are from Java, in Asia. They are made of wood and used to tell stories. A puppeteer works them by moving the long sticks attached to their bodies.

△The Aborigine people in Australia tell their children wonderful stories as they paint Dreamtime pictures. The children learn to paint the pictures and remember the stories so they can tell them to their own children one day. This way, the stories will never be forgotten.

▷For hundreds of years, people have ridden horses to round up their cattle in America. Today, cowgirls and cowboys show off their horse-riding skills to crowds of people at shows called rodeos. They are popular in the United States and Canada.

449

# The Americas

For hundreds of years, the Americas have drawn people from all over the world. Amazing landscapes and different climates still attract millions of visitors each year. Some decide to stay after their holiday. All of these peoples add to the richness and colourful style of American life.

△ The area called the Americas is shown in red.

▽ Holidaymakers love to visit the Grand Canyon in the United States. The Colorado River carved out its deep valleys over millions of years.

Colorado River

△ Many people go to see the famous Statue of Liberty, in New York City.

▷ Fruit and vegetables are sold in this busy market, high in the Andes mountains.

△ The Horseshoe Falls in Canada are part of the group of waterfalls called Niagara Falls. Some of the falls are in Canada, the rest are in the United States.

▽ Sugar Loaf mountain rises above the bay in Rio de Janeiro, Brazil. The city is a lively place to live, surrounded by magnificent views.

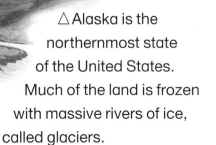

△ Alaska is the northernmost state of the United States. Much of the land is frozen with massive rivers of ice, called glaciers.

**Word box**
**Glaciers** are huge rivers of ice that move very slowly down valleys. They follow the easiest way to the sea.
**Canyons** are deep, steep-sided valleys. They are usually in dry areas where the sides do not get worn away by the beating rain.

451

# The frozen north

The Inuit people came from Asia to Canada thousands of years ago. The early Inuits used dog sleds for transport and made homes from snow or animal skins. There was no soil for growing food, so they hunted caribou and seals for food and clothing. Today, some Inuits hunt, but most work in offices and factories.

### How Ishdaka found Summer
(An Inuit folk tale)

There was once a time when a giant called Winter ruled Ishdaka's northern land, keeping it frozen all year round. Ishdaka travelled south to ask Summer for her help. She agreed, and together they tricked Winter and were able to melt all the ice and snow.

Thereafter, the giant only ruled for part of the year, so that Summer had a chance to visit and bring warmth to Ishdaka's people.

△ Rubbing noses is an Inuit sign of affection, like a kiss.

◁ Inuits catch fish to eat. This man is spearing fish through an ice hole.

▷Today, most Inuits live in wooden houses and drive snow mobiles and cars. Planes bring supplies and medicines.

snow mobile

# Native Americans

Native Americans were the first people to live in North America. They spoke many languages and hunted, fished and farmed. When Europeans arrived, Native Americans were forced to live in areas known as reservations.

△ The Pueblo people are Native Americans. They dance and sing at the maize festival to make the rains come and bring them a good harvest.

▷ The medicine man uses magic to help heal sick people. He draws magic signs in the sand and chants.

▽ White settlers from Europe first arrived over 350 years ago. At first, they were friends with the Native Americans, but later fought many wars against them.

**Find the answers**

Who were the first people to live in North America?

What does the medicine man use to help heal people?

# Forestry

British Columbia in Canada is one of the world's largest timber producers. Timber is wood from trees. It is needed to make building materials, furniture and paper.

The Columbian forests are looked after carefully, so that new tree seedlings are always growing to replace the trees that are cut down.

△ Trees are cut down by forest workers called lumberjacks. They use power saws.

△ Huge trucks take the trees away to sawmills. Then the bark is removed from the trees and they are sawn into planks.

◁ Trunks of maple trees are drilled to collect a watery sap. When this is boiled it turns into the sweet, sticky liquid known as maple syrup.

**Find the answers**

What is made from timber?

Where is British Columbia?

▷ Maple syrup is delicious on waffles and pancakes.

# Cattle ranches

North American farmers keep cattle on big farms called ranches. Cattle over nine months old are kept in fenced off areas and fed on special food to make them grow bigger. Lassos are used to round up the cattle.

◁ The South American cowboy is called a gaucho. He wears a broad hat, baggy trousers, a decorated belt and spurs on his boots.

spurs

**Make a gaucho hat**

Cut a circle of card with a hole the size of your head. Cut a strip of card 4 cm wide, to make a headband. Cut edges of band, as shown. Tape ends to fit your head. Fold bottom edges and glue over hole. Cut a circle the size of your headband and glue on top.

▽ Cattle in North America have been rounded up on horseback since the early days of the Wild West.

lasso

◁ On some large ranches, trucks and helicopters are used to find lost cattle.

# West Indies

The West Indies is made up of thousands of islands in the Caribbean Sea. Cuba is the largest of these islands.

Bananas, coconuts, coffee, cotton, tobacco and sugar cane grow well in the warm weather on these islands.

It is sunny all year round, so people can work and relax outside.

▽ Puerto Rico is an island in the West Indies. Puerto Rican fishermen go out to sea in small boats. They often have to mend nets that have ripped on rocks below the sea.

**Make Caribbean bananas**

Peel some bananas. Ask an adult to cut them into two. For each, mix two tablespoons of orange juice with a teaspoon of lemon juice and two teaspoons of brown sugar. Pour on top. Sprinkle a tablespoon of coconut over each. Ask an adult to grill them for five minutes.

**Find the answers**

Which is the largest island in the West Indies?

What grows well in the West Indies?

# Amazon Indians

Amazon Indians live in the South American rainforests. They look after the forest because it gives them all the food, medicine and building materials they need.

Other people are not looking after the land. They are cutting down many of the trees to sell as timber or to make space for new farms.

## How the birds got their colours
*(A South American folk tale)*

*Once all birds were white, until a wicked rainbow snake was killed. The cormorant who had killed the snake was supposed to have its skin as a prize, but he was told it was only his if he could carry it. All the birds helped, and were given the piece of skin they had carried. Their feathers changed to similar colours, and are the same today.*

▽ Many Amazon Indians sleep in hammocks and cook food outside.

△ These men are fishing with a bow and arrow. They must have sharp eyes and move quickly to catch fish this way.

◁ The forest people live in clearings. They get all their food from the forest and rivers. Hunters often go away for many days at a time.

457

# Mexico

More people live in Mexico City, Mexico's busy capital, than in any other city in the world. Other Mexican towns are quieter, especially during the hottest part of the day, when most people rest.

Many visitors travel to Mexico to see the amazing temples that were built by the Aztecs.

△ The Aztecs lived in Mexico hundreds of years ago. Their capital, Tenochtitlán, probably looked like this. The ruins of these temples are visited by people today.

▽ It is noon, the hottest part of the day, in this small Mexican town. Many people have gone inside to rest, away from the sun. Others take a break from their work and sit in the shade under the cool arches in the town square.

**Find the answers**

What is Mexico's capital city?

Why do most people rest at noon?

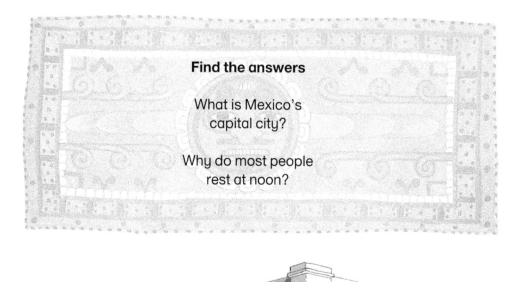

# Traditions

Carnival, Thanksgiving and the Canadian Winter Festival are just a few of the many traditions that take place in the Americas today. They are happy times, when people celebrate with their friends, family and neighbours.

△ Each year, a giant ice palace is built for the Winter Festival in Quebec, Canada.

△ Carnival is a famous and colourful street festival. It takes place in Rio de Janeiro, Brazil, every year. People parade and dance in bright costumes.

▷ Thanksgiving is the United State's favourite tradition. The first Thanksgiving was a huge party thrown by settlers, to thank the Native Americans for showing them how to farm their new land.

# Europe

Europe is made up of many countries. The northernmost areas in the Arctic are cold and snowy all year round. In the south, by the Mediterranean Sea, it can be very hot and dry.

People from northern Europe, such as Scandinavia, are often fair skinned with light hair. People from southern Europe, such as Italy, are usually darker.

△ Europe's many countries make up the red shape shown on this map.

◁ People from all over the world visit the Mediterranean countries to lie in the sun on sandy beaches and swim in the warm, blue sea.

▽ Iceland has many geysers. They blast hot water into the air, every now and then.

△ Some Sami, or Lapp people, keep reindeer. They take them further south in the spring. On the way, they live in tents called lavos.

▷St Basil's church in Moscow, Russia, is famous for its many brightly coloured, onion-shaped domes. Russia is such a large country, that it stretches across both Europe and Asia. Moscow is in Europe.

▽ Prague, the capital of the Czech Republic, is full of many old and beautiful buildings. It is called the city of 100 spires because it has so many churches.

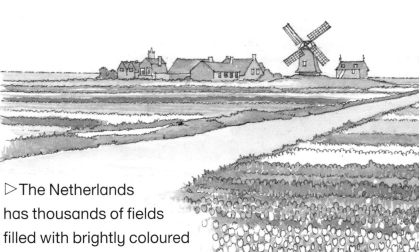

▷The Netherlands has thousands of fields filled with brightly coloured tulips that are sold abroad.

△ Edinburgh Castle in Scotland stands high above the city on a volcanic rock.

**Word box**
**Geysers** are hot springs that throw up jets of hot water. In volcanic areas, hot water underground turns to steam and pushes out into the air. **Mediterranean** areas include all the lands surrounding the Mediterranean Sea.

461

# Farming

Some European farmers keep animals, others grow crops, many do both.

Machines can be used to plant and harvest crops on flatter land. Farming hilly ground is more difficult. These areas are often used to graze sheep and goats.

**Make a sheep picture**
Draw a sheep using this shape as a guide. Colour in its face and legs. Glue cotton wool onto its back. Glue used match sticks to make a sheep pen, as shown.

▽ A lot of wheat is grown in Europe. Tractors and combine harvesters gather in the crop towards the end of summer.

△ On a small farm, everyone helps to look after the animals. The chickens are given grain to eat and their eggs are collected each day.

△ Many farms in Spain grow grapes. The grapes are cut in September, and are mostly made into wine.

# Fishing

The fishing industry in Europe is huge. Thousands of tons of fish are sent to the fish markets every day.

Shellfish, such as lobsters and crabs, are trapped in baskets. Other fish are caught by floating nets.

**Find the answers**

What are large fishing boats called?

How are shellfish caught?

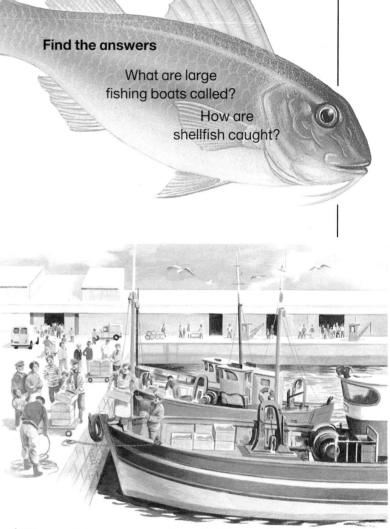

▽ Fishing is often a family business. These two Greek brothers fish every day. Sometimes they hire out their boat to holidaymakers.

△ These fishermen are from Brittany, in France. They go out to sea for several days in large boats. They sell the fish they catch in a fish market in their home port.

▷ Large fishing boats are called trawlers. The fishermen on this Russian trawler will freeze the fish on board to keep it fresh until they return.

# Mountains

Europe has many beautiful mountains. In Norway, inlets of sea, called fjords, cut into mountainous coastlines. The world-famous Alps stretch through many countries. Hundreds of people climb and ski on them every year.

**Dogs to the rescue!**
The St Bernard dog is named after the St Bernard monastery in the Swiss Alps. Many years ago, the monks in this monastery reared and trained these dogs to rescue people trapped on the mountains in snow blizzards.

▷The countries of Scandinavia have warm summers. People on holiday sometimes bathe in low mountain lakes. They also take special baths, called saunas, inside wooden cabins.

◁These people have come to a ski resort for their holiday. Those who are used to skiing will climb the mountain in a chair lift and ski down. Beginners will ski on gentle slopes, or practise on flatter areas in the resort's village. Others prefer to sled or toboggan.

# Traditions

As Europe is made up of so many countries, there are hundreds of different festivals and celebrations.

Certain festivals, such as New Year, are celebrated by groups of people everywhere. Some traditions belong to one area or country only.

△ In Switzerland, there is an opening parade every autumn for the onion festival.

△ In Italy, over 300 years ago, a puppet called Pulcinella became so well loved, the show spread to France. From there it went to England, where Pulcinella became Mr Punch.

△ Russian dancing is famous throughout the world. The dancers have to be very fit and strong. They kick their legs out while squatting, leap high in the air and touch their toes.

# Africa

Africa is an area of many landscapes and climates. It includes tropical rainforests and the world's largest and hottest desert, the Sahara.

Three-quarters of Africans live in the countryside, earning their living by farming. More and more people are moving to the cities to work in shops, offices and factories.

△ Africa is shown in red. It is made up of many countries.

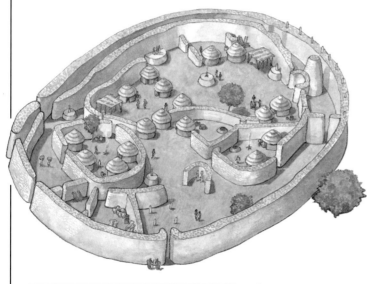

◁ About 900 years ago, the Shona people built the city of Great Zimbabwe in southern Africa. Its ruins are still there today.

**Word box**
**Safaris** are journeys into the wild to see and photograph wild animals in their natural surroundings.
**Pyramids** were built in Egypt thousands of years ago as places to bury important people when they died.

▷ In Morocco, north Africa, the old part of some towns have walls around them. Souks, or town markets, are within these walls.

◁ In ancient Egypt, Pharaohs, or kings, were buried in pyramid tombs with their treasure.

▽ There are many open markets in west Africa. These women are carrying the shopping home on their heads.

△ Some African towns are on rivers, so boats can be used to carry people and goods.

△ Once people on safari shot large African animals. Nowadays, they take photographs instead.

# Village and nomadic life

In the towns, many people live in modern houses built from manufactured materials. In the villages, houses are often made of sun-dried mud with roofs of straw or leaves.

Tuareg and Masai people do not live in towns or villages. They live a nomadic life, which means they travel from place to place.

△ This Tuareg man is lowering a bucket on a rope to scoop water from a well below the desert sand.

▽ The Tuareg people wander the Sahara Desert with their camels and goats. Their homes are tents carried on the camels' backs.

△ Camels are used to carry goods across the desert. They can travel for days without a drink.

### Snake magic
(A folk tale from east Africa)

*A poor, hungry woman and her son helped a snake. They were rewarded with a magic ring and a casket that always gave them a home, riches and delicious food.*

△ In many African villages, women prepare meals together outside their homes. They pound millet or cassava into flour.

▷ The greatest day in a young Masai warrior's life is when he becomes a junior elder. Young women dress up in colourful beaded collars for the warrior's procession.

△ Bridges made from branches and vines cross some rivers. They look wobbly, but local people use them easily.

◁ Masai women build a holy house, called an osinkira, for the young warrior's ceremony. An altar inside it is made from three wooden stakes cut from sacred trees. The house is always burned afterwards.

# Farming

In some parts of Africa modern machinery is used to farm the land, but most farmers use simple tools. In eastern and southern grassland areas, peanuts, maize and millet are grown. In warm, wet areas, bananas, rice and yams grow well. Coffee, cocoa beans, coconuts and cotton are grown mainly to sell abroad.

△ Ostriches are very strong and can be ridden like horses. They can give a nasty kick if they are in a bad mood!

△ Ostriches are kept in South Africa for their eggs, feathers and meat. The females have special shelters where they lay their eggs.

▽ In Zaire, central Africa, the farmers grow tea bushes on hillsides. The leaves are picked by hand. They are dried before being packed.

▽ Coffee plants produce fruits called berries. Each berry has two beans. Some of these are roasted and ground to make coffee powder.

**Find the answers**

Why are ostriches kept in South Africa?

In which part of Africa are peanuts grown?

▽ Some farmers are lucky enough to have land near Africa's longest river, the river Nile. Waterwheel pumps, worked by animals, keep the Nile's water flowing along ditches to water crops.

**Make an ostrich**
Draw an ostrich onto card, using this shape as a guide. Colour it in. Glue on a bead for its eye.

Cut out feather shapes from black and white paper. Cut edges, as shown. Glue the feathers onto your ostrich's body.

# Life on the water

Some people in Africa live in villages by the sea and rivers. There are few streets, but people move about easily in small boats.

The houses are built on high stilts, so that when the river rises during the rainy season, the houses are kept dry. Children here are more used to water than dry land!

**Make a stilt house**
Cut and fold the ends of four tubes, as shown. Tape to the bottom of a cardboard box. Fold a piece of card in half. Tape over box to make roof. Paint doors and windows. Glue straws onto the roof.

▷ This is a fishing village in Benin, west Africa. Local people can buy vegetables and fruit from boats that visit their homes.

**The pumpkin boat**
(A folk tale from Madagascar)

One day a pumpkin fell into the river. A group of small animals thought it would make a wonderful boat to sail down river. But Rat became hungry and secretly began to nibble the bottom. When water flooded in, the boat tipped over and all the animals had to swim for the shore. They were all very angry with Rat!

# Traditions

Many of the African countries are famous for their traditional crafts. Beautiful masks and colourful materials have been made in the same way for thousands of years.

There are also exciting festivals and celebrations all over Africa.

△ This colourful cloth is from Ghana in west Africa. It is woven from dyed cotton. Traditional clothes in Africa often have bright colours and bold patterns.

◁ African people have made masks out of materials such as clay, wood, bronze and gold for thousands of years. This mask was made in central Africa. It was used for special ceremonies.

◁ Every year, men from Argungu in Nigeria hold a fishing festival. They fish for giant perches, using dried gourds, or calabashes, as floats.

473

# Asia

Asia covers a vast area. Its lands vary from freezing Siberia in the north to warm, tropical India and Thailand in the southeast.

Over half of the people in the world live in Asia. Many of them live in busy cities. Very few people live in the dry desert and rocky mountain areas.

△ Asia's enormous land area is shown in red.

▷ Many people living in the Middle East are Muslim. They worship in a mosque, like this one in Dubai. It looks spectacular when it is lit up at night.

▽ These Hindus are bathing in the holy waters of the river Ganges in Varanasi, northern India.

△ Over half of Thailand is covered in teak forest. Teak is a very important timber tree. Elephants move the teak logs to the river, where they are floated down to the sawmills in the capital city, Bangkok.

◁ There are many bazaars, or markets, in Afghanistan. People from the hills and mountains come to sell their goods.

△ China's city streets are busy. Bicycles are often the quickest way to travel around.

△ The Himalayas are the highest mountain range in the world. Many people try to climb them every year.

◁ The Great Wall of China was built over 1,000 years ago to protect China. It is the longest wall in the world.

**Word box**
**Teak** timber comes from forests in Southeast Asia. It polishes well, so is used to make furniture.
**Bazaars** are eastern markets where goods are sold or swapped.

# Different ways of life

Most Asian people live and work in villages, towns or cities, but some people choose to lead a different way of life. This may be because they have special beliefs, such as the Buddhist monks. Other people, such as some Mongolian and Tibetan families travel around to work. A few of the unusual ways of life in Asia are shown on this page.

△ These people are from Mongolia. They wander the grassy plains with their animals. Their homes are felt tents, called yurts.

◁ On the slopes of the Himalayan mountains, Buddhist monks live in monasteries. They have chosen to live apart from other people, so they can pray and study in peace.

▷In Israel there are farms called kibbutzim. Everyone works together to grow food for the people of the kibbutz and to sell at markets. Here, workers are picking oranges.

◁This is a whole village under one roof. The Iban people of Sarawak, Malaysia, often live in a longhouse like this. Inside, as many as 70 families have separate rooms, off a long corridor.

◁In Chang Tang, Tibet, some families live in tents made of yak skin. They sell salt to China. These bags have been filled from a salt pan and are ready for the long trek back to camp.

477

# Industry

People who manufacture, or make, similar products are said to work in the same industry. There are a huge number of industries in Asia. Some Asian industries make very complicated electrical goods. Others are simple industries, such as farming rice, cotton and tea.

△ Rice grows best in flooded fields, so all of the work has to be done by hand or with the help of animals.

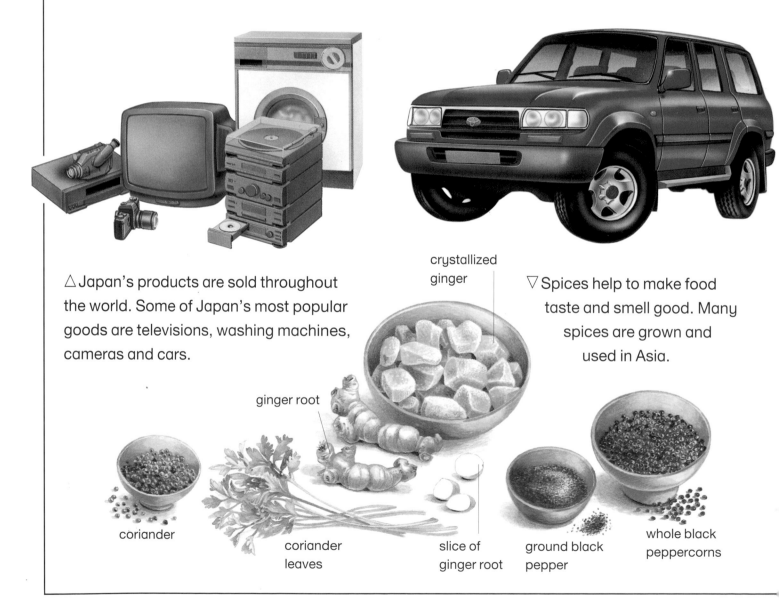

△ Japan's products are sold throughout the world. Some of Japan's most popular goods are televisions, washing machines, cameras and cars.

crystallized ginger

▽ Spices help to make food taste and smell good. Many spices are grown and used in Asia.

ginger root

coriander

coriander leaves

slice of ginger root

ground black pepper

whole black peppercorns

△ Oil is one of Asia's biggest industries. Over half the world's oil is found in Asia, with a quarter of it mined in Saudi Arabia alone.

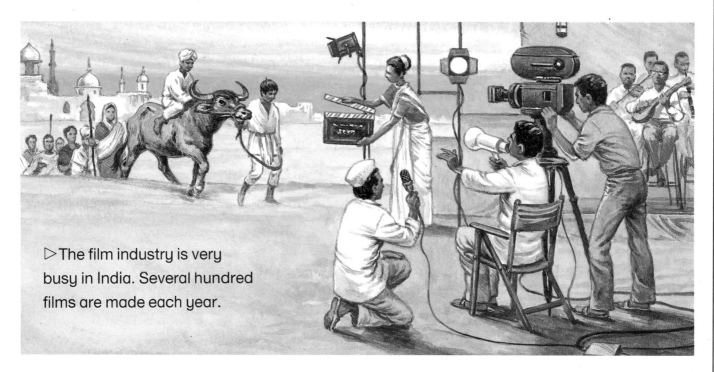

▷ The film industry is very busy in India. Several hundred films are made each year.

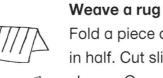

**Weave a rug**

Fold a piece of thin card in half. Cut slits, as shown. Open out. Tape strips of coloured paper to one edge. Weave strips in and out until you reach the end. Tape in place. Weave strips until you have a colourful rug.

▽ Woven Persian rugs are famous around the world.

# Traditions

There are many celebrations and traditions to be found throughout the different countries in Asia. All are fun to watch or take part in. You can see people dressing up in costumes, an exciting fireworks display and a colourful painting on these pages. Perhaps you have been lucky enough to see some of them before.

△ Islamic art is based on the Muslim religion. Many beautiful patterns and designs are created.

▽ During the Chinese New Year, some adults dress in a dragon costume and dance through the streets collecting gifts for those in need.

480

▽ On the island of Bali, in Indonesia, the women and children offer gifts of flowers and fruit to the gods, to help protect their villages.

**Make a Bun Bang Fai picture**

Draw a firework picture with wax crayons. Use your brightest colours and draw plenty of rockets. Place it on an old newspaper and cover your picture with black paint. Watch what happens to your fireworks.

▷ In Thailand, villagers hold a festival called Bun Bang Fai, to make sure the rains come. They light enormous rockets.

◁ The Kabuki theatre, in Japan, began over 300 years ago. All the parts were played by men. Many Kabuki plays are still performed in Japan today.

△ The Japanese tea ceremony teaches that even everyday actions should be thought about deeply.

481

# Australasia and the Pacific Islands

Australasia's largest countries are Australia, Papua New Guinea and New Zealand. In the Pacific Ocean there are thousands of islands that we call the Pacific Islands. Some are too tiny to see on a map. Over this enormous area, there are hot deserts, cold mountains and warm tropical seas.

△ Australasia and the Pacific Islands cover the enormous red area shown above.

▷The Sydney Opera House, Australia, is a very famous landmark. It was built to look like sailing boats in the harbour. The bridge behind it links north and south Sydney, the largest city in Australia.

▽ Wellington is the capital of New Zealand. The city is famous for its steep hills and its very strong winds.

**Word box**
**National Parks** are large, protected areas where wildlife can live in safety.
**Reefs** are ridges of coral that build up below the surface of the sea.
**Aborigines** are people who lived in Australia long before Europeans arrived.

◁ Fjordland is a National Park along the southwest coast of New Zealand. It is a protected area, so people are not allowed to build on it. It is known for its beautiful mountains and scenery.

▷ The Great Barrier Reef, off the Australian coast, is the largest coral reef in the world. Thousands of tourists visit the colourful coral reef each year.

▽ Uluru, or Ayers Rock, is sacred to the Australian Aborigines. Its caves are covered with ancient paintings.

▷ These giant stone statues are on Easter Island in Polynesia. No one knows who carved them. Traditional stories tell of the statues walking to their resting place, helped by a magical power.

483

# Farming and industry

The farm and factory products from Australasia and the Pacific Islands are very popular in other countries. Japan is one of the main buyers of goods from Australia, New Zealand and Papua New Guinea.

New Zealand has more sheep than people. The sheep are sold worldwide.

△ Sheep shearers in New Zealand often travel from farm to farm. Some can shear a sheep in under a minute!

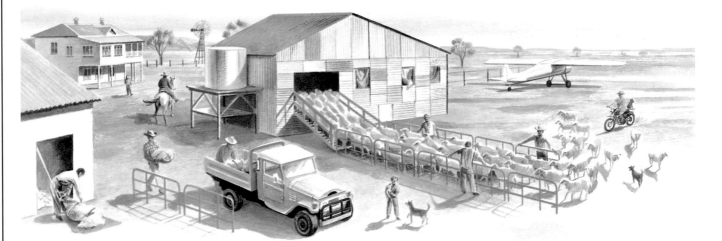

△ Australian sheep farms are so large that farmers use planes and trucks to get around them. At shearing time, sheep are driven into sheds to have their wool cut off.

◁ Sugar is the island of Fiji's most important crop. Many people earn their living by working on sugar plantations.

▷One of the world's largest copper mines is on the island of Bougainville, Papua New Guinea. Apart from the pure copper sold, small amounts of gold also come from this mine.

**Find the answers**

What is an opal?

What is Fiji's most important crop?

△South Australia grows lots of grapes that are used for making wine. It is so popular that many thousands of litres are sold at home and abroad every year.

△Almost all the world's opals come from Australia. Opals are milky-coloured gemstones with other threads of colour in them. They are used in jewellery, such as rings and bracelets.

485

# Australian traditions

The first people settled in Australia about 40,000 years ago. These people were called Aborigines. Although many Aboriginal people now live in cities, there are a number who live in the outback, or areas of wilderness. These people have followed their own traditions for thousands of years.

Many Australians came from Europe and Asia and still follow the traditions of their original countries.

△ This is a didgeridoo. It is a musical instrument which makes a long, droning sound, like a loud bee. Didgeridoos play the background sound to many Aborigine songs.

**Make a rock painting**
Stuff a large, strong paper bag with newspaper and seal top edges with sticky tape. Paste glue over the front. Cover with sand. Leave to dry. Draw simple stick figures and animals with wax crayons on sandy side.

△ Paintings and carvings created thousands of years ago, can be seen on rocks and in caves today. Many of them tell old Aborigine stories.

▷Aborigines have used boomerangs for hunting and sport for thousands of years. If thrown properly, they come right back to the thrower.

◁This camel race is part of a big sports day. Watching and taking part in sports competitions is an important part of Australian life.

▷Australians enjoy outdoor life. On a sunny day, people often put on sunscreen cream and go to the seaside. Surfing is a favourite sport.

# Island traditions

Early Polynesians were adventurous sailors. They braved the unknown seas in small, light boats, searching for new lands. Finally, they settled on many of the Pacific Islands.

Traditions were handed down from family to family and are still part of everyday life today.

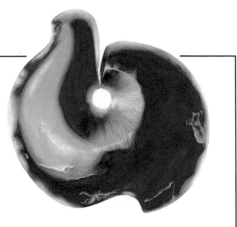

△ Amulets, or lucky pendants, have been worn by Maori people for hundreds of years. This one is worn, or placed in the water while fishing, to help the owner catch many fish.

◁ In Papua New Guinea, men hold meetings and ceremonies in spirit houses called Haus Tambarans. These have life-size wooden figures, or spirits, that watch over the village.

▷ Hawaiian dancing is called hula. Hula dancers have special costumes and often wear garlands around their necks. Stories are chanted while the dancing takes place.

# Index

This index will help you to find out where you can read information about a subject. It is in alphabetical order. Each section is under a large letter of the alphabet. A main entry and its page numbers are printed in **dark**, or **bold**, letters. This is where you will find the most information. Below a main entry, there may be a second list. This shows other places in the book where you can find further information on your subject.

**The publishers would like to thank the following artists for their contribution to this book:**

Hemesh Alles (Maggie Mundy Agency Ltd); Jonathan Adams; Marion Appleton; Mike Atkinson (Garden Studio Illustrators Agents); Craig Austin; Graham Austin; Janet Baker; Julian Baker; Bob Bampton; Julie Banyard; John Barber; Shirley Barker (Artist Partners Ltd); Denise Bazin; Tim Beer (Maggie Mundy Agency Ltd); Pierre Bon; Maggie Brand; Derek Brazell; Brihton Illustration Agency; Peter Bull Art Studios; John Butler; Vanessa Card; Diana Catchpole (Linda Rogers Associates); Jonathan Cate; David Cook (Linden Artists); Bob Corley (Artist Partners Ltd); Joanne Cowne; Jim Channell; Caroline Jayne Church; Peter Dennis (Linda Rogers Associates); Kay Dixey; Maggie Downer; Richard Draper; Bernard Duhem; Jean-Philippe Duponq; David Eddington (Maggie Mundy Agency Ltd); Luc Favreau; Diane Fawcett; Catherine Fichaux; Michael Fisher; Roy Flooks; Chris Forsey; Rosamund Fowler (Artist Partners Ltd); Andrew French; Tony Gibbons; Mick Gillah; Peter Goodfellow; Matthew Gore; Ray Grinaway; Terry Hadler; Rebecca Hardy; Nick Hawken; Tim Hayward; Ron Haywood; Pierre Hezard; Kay Hodges; Stephen Holmes; Mark Iley; Ian Jackson; John James; Rhian Nest James (Maggie Mundy Agency Ltd); Ron Jobson; Kevin Jones Associates; David Kearney; Pete Kelly; Roger Kent (Garden Studio Illustrators Agents); Tony Kenyon; Kevin Kimber (B.L. Kearley Ltd); Deborah Kindred; Stuart Lafford (Linden Artists); Marc Lagarde; Terence Lambert; Stephen Lings (Linden Artists); Bernard Long (Temple Rogers Artists Agents); John Lupton (Linden Artists); Gilbert Macé; Kevin Maddison; Alan Male (Linden Artists); Shirley Mallinson; Maltings Partnership; Josephine Martin (Garden Studio Illustrators Agents); Barry Mitchell; Robert Morton; Patrick Mulrey; David McAllister; Dee McClean (Linden Artists); Polly Noakes (Linda Rogers Associates); Steve Noon (Garden Studio Illustrators Agents); Oxford Illustrators; Darren Pattenden (Garden Studio Illustrators Agents); Jean-Marc Pau; Bruce Pearson; Jane Pickering (Linden Artists); Stephen Player; Sebastian Quigley (Linden Artists); Bernard Robinson; Eric Robson; Michael Roffe; Michelle Ross (Linden Artists); Eric Rowe (Linden Artists); Susan Rowe (Garden Studio Illustrators Agents); Martin Salisbury; Danièle Schulthess; Stephen Seymour; Brian Smith; Guy Smith (Mainline Design); Lesley Smith (John Martin and Artists); Étienne Souppart; John Spires; Clive Spong (Linden Artists); Valérie Stetton; Roger Stewart (Kevin Jones Associates); Tess Stone; Swanston Graphics; Eva Styner; Treve Tamblin (John Martin and Artists); Jean Torton; Shirley Tourret (B.L. Kearley Ltd); Simon Tegg; Guy Troughton; Michèle Trumel; Visage Design; Vincent Wakely; Ross Watton (Garden Studio Illustrators Agents); Phil Weare (Linden Artists); Graham White; Joanna Williams; Ann Winterbotham; David Wright

**The publishers wish to thank the following for supplying photographs for this book:**

Page 47 Hergé/Casterman; 60 Frederick Warne & Co, 1902, 1987; 122 Mary Evans Picture Library; 145 National Maritime Museum, Greenwich; 162 Mansell Collection; 169 BATMAN is a trademark of DC Comics © 1991. All Rights Reserved. Reprinted by permission of DC Comics; 206 Mary Evans Picture Library; 222 Victoria & Albert Museum, London/Bridgeman Art Library; 226 Private Collection/Bridgeman Art Library; 233 1973 by E.H. Shepard and Methuen Children's Books Ltd; 250 Ronald Grant Archive; 252 Ronald Grant Archive; 299 Mansell Collection; 302 Ronald Grant Archive/DC Comics; 306 Mary Evans Picture Library; 311 Ronald Grant Archive; 341 Mary Evans Picture Library; 374 'Thunderbirds' I.T.C. Entertainment Group Ltd; 425 Ronald Grant Archive

Thanks also to photographer David Rudkin and models Felicity Lea and Kane Tunmore of Scallywags; and to the World Conservation Monitoring Centre for their kind help